SOTHIS PRESS

Sothis Press aims to completely reimagine the public domain book with an emphasis on universal access to captivatingly designed print editions. We believe that technology will enable every single book ever published to be perpetually accessible in beautiful print form. Sothis is beauty in ubiquity.

www.sothis.press
1 Waterhouse Square, London, ECIN 2ST

Freight Claims

William A. Trimpe

SOTHIS PRESS

ISBN 978-1-0368-0037-6

Freight Claims is in the
public domain.

This edition is published by
Sothis Press © 2023. The company
is registered in England and Wales.
The Company Number is 14900389.

FREIGHT CLAIMS

WILLIAM A. TRIMPE, A. B., LL. B.
Of the Chicago Bar

La Salle Extension University
· Chicago ·
1920

(4-150)

CONTENTS

FREIGHT CLAIMS

I. FOREWORD AND SCOPE OF THIS TREATISE

1. Foreword

There is probably no point of contact between the common carriers of the country and the shipping public which has given rise to more controversy and has been the cause of more dissatisfaction with the carriers than that arising out of the collection of what are commonly called "freight claims." It is probably just as true that there ought to be no transaction between the shipping public and the carriers easier of adjustment than such claims.

There was a time in the history of American railroads when the claim department was the only one in the efficiency of which the carrier had little or no interest, except in its ability to pay as few claims as possible, and in what is known in the vernacular as "stalling off" the remainder until the claimant, despairing of ever securing redress, abandoned the attempt. Needless to say, this attitude upon the part of the carriers was not productive of sympathetic and cordial relations between them and their customers, the shipping public.

Fortunately for all concerned, there has been, within

the decade just past, a radical change in the attitude of the carriers upon the subject of claims. The enormous sums of money which carriers have and are paying out every year on claims, the constant annoying friction between shipper and carrier in addition to the serious financial aspects of the situation, have brought about a realization that the manner in which claims are handled has a direct and important bearing on the attitude of the shipping public toward the carrier, and thus very directly on the success or failure of the struggle of the various lines and systems to retain old and acquire new business. Many other causes, a discussion of which is impossible and unnecessary in this treatise, have contributed to the result that at the present time the carriers of the country, on the whole, are making an honest and efficient endeavor to handle claims expeditiously, and with a view toward bringing about a fair determination and adjustment of the rights of the parties.

It has been stated above that of the various questions arising between the shipper and the carrier none should be easier of adjustment than a claim by the shipper against the carrier for loss, damage, or overcharge to freight. The reason is that when the carrier accepts a shipment for transportation, it thereupon undertakes to transport that shipment from the point of origin to the point of destination, within a reasonable time, and to deliver the shipment in good condition (or at least in the same condition as received). This is done under a clear and explicit contract which, taken with the duties and obligations placed upon it by law, governs and controls where there is a breach by either party.

Now, if during the course of transportation the shipment is lost or damaged or there is delay which gives rise to damage, or if the charge for the service performed is incorrect, or unlawful, it simply devolves upon the shipper or the consignee, as the case may be, to present to the carrier, in the form of a claim, the facts, in proper form and properly verified, together with a statement of the damage incurred, so that the carrier may have before it all the relevant matters necessary to investigate and verify the alleged breach of its contract of carriage and to determine its liability therefor. A claim and the facts with reference thereto being placed before the carrier, it usually is an easy matter for it to investigate and verify the facts set up by the claimant as constituting a breach of the carrier's contract; and then, having the facts before it, to determine whether or not the claim is one which it is under any obligation to pay. Of course, the determination of this question involves legal questions as to whether or not the facts in the claim constitute a breach of the carrier's contract for which it is liable to the shipper, and the further questions, the breach of the contract being established, of the amount of the damage and how it is to be ascertained or computed.

2. Scope of this Treatise

A discussion of the latter questions is entirely without the scope of this treatise. Such a discussion will be found in the treatise on "Law of Carriers of Goods," which constitutes a part of this course. The object of this treatise is to explain the proper manner of making up, presenting, and collecting claims against common carriers, involving loss, damage, or overcharge to shipments. We start with the assumption that the shipper has a valid claim against the carrier for violation of the contract of carriage, and is concerned merely with presenting, in non-technical form, the nature and contents of the various documents which should be filed in substantiation of a claim and the reasons why these documents are necessary, together with suggestions with reference to what might be called the tactics of handling freight claims.[1]

It must, therefore, be clear at the outset that this is not primarily a legal treatise on the relation between the shipper and the carrier, or a discussion of the various duties, rights, and remedies arising therefrom; and, therefore, *such statements of law as it may be necessary to make in order to explain the various steps involved in properly presenting a claim will, of necessity, be general in their character and must not be taken to be a full and complete exposition of the subject matter.* Neither is it within the scope of this treatise to discuss various other matters more or less intimately related to the preparation and collection of freight claims, as, for example, measures of prevention both upon the part of the carrier and of the shipper, the proper description of freight shipments, the packing and handling of freight, and the checking of shipments, rates, tariffs, and classifications. These subjects, and others similarly related more or less directly to the subject of this treatise, are covered in other treatises in this course.

[1] For the benefit of the reader who may not have seen a freight claim, we show in Appendix A of this treatise, some of the documents and correspondence in connection with the handling of a typical claim. We would suggest that the reader refer to this appendix from time to time in reading the requirements for the handling of claims here set forth, bearing in mind, of course, that every claim is somewhat different from every other claim and that circumstances alter the procedure in the adjustment of even claims which seem to be identical.

II. CLAIMS FOR LOSS

1. Total Loss of Shipment

Claims for total loss of a shipment arise where, after the shipment has been tendered and accepted by the carrier and a bill of lading issued therefor, in the course of the transportation the shipment becomes wholly lost so that the carrier is unable to make delivery; or where, during the course of the transportation, the shipment is either wholly destroyed or is so damaged as to make it worthless. (See Sections 20 and 21, Pomerene Law.)

(a) By Whom Claim May Be Presented

A claim for total loss should be presented by (1) *the consignor,* where the consignor is still the owner of the shipment, that is, where the title to the shipment has not been transferred to the consignee at the time of delivery of the shipment to the carrier, or (2) *the consignee,* where the title to the shipment is in the consignee and where the consignee is the owner of the shipment.

The general rule is, that delivery to the carrier, in the absence of notice to the contrary, is presumed to be delivery to the consignee; that is to say, the consignee is presumed to be the owner of the goods and, therefore, is entitled to present a claim. It is important in presenting claims that the claimant's right and title to the goods and, therefore, his right to present the claim, be established. Ordinarily, possession of the bill of lading, properly endorsed where an endorsement would be necessary to explain its possession, is an indication of ownership, although possession of a bill of lading is not conclusive. The statutes of many states require the carrier to deliver the shipment to whoever presents the original bill of lading in proper form.[2]

(b) Documents Filed in Support of Claim

A claim for total loss should be supported by (1) *the original bill of lading* or, if the claimant is unable for any reason to present the original bill of lading, by (2) *a bond of indemnity.* In the event that the claim is recognized and paid and the original bill of lading is later presented by some other party, the carrier, being required by law to honor the original bill of lading in the hands of the holder, would be put in the position of having to pay the claim twice. The bond is required to protect the carrier against this contingency. A copy of this bond is shown below.

LONG FORM OF INDEMNIFYING BOND*

Know All Men by These Presents, that we, ..., of the City of.............., State of............, as Principal, and.............., of the City of.............., State of................, as Surety, are held and firmly bound unto.....................Railroad Company in the penal sum of............Dollars, lawful money of the United States, for the payment of which sum, well and truly to be made, we bind ourselves, our successors and assigns or our heirs, executors and administrators jointly, severally and firmly by these presents.

Witness our hands and seals this.......day of............, 19....

The Condition of the Above Obligation is Such that whereas on the........day of................ 19.., there was delivered to the said.....................Railroad Company at ...., State of..........., by................., a shipment of.... ....for transportation by said Railroad Company to.............., State of..............; and,

[2] Some phases of the carriers' liability are treated in the Pomerene Bill of Lading Law, which became effective January 1, 1917. This law will be found reproduced in Appendix D.

WHEREAS said shipment while in possession of said carrier and before delivery was.................... ; and,
(lost or damaged)

WHEREAS said......................desires to file a claim against the said....................Railroad Company in the sum of..........Dollars covering said....................,
(loss or damage)
but is unable to present with said claim the original Bill of Lading covering said shipment.

Now if the said....................................shall
(Names of Principal and Surety)
and do from time to time and at all times hereafter, defend, save, keep harmless and indemnify said.................... Railroad Company aforesaid, its successors, assigns, agents and attorneys, and all and each of them of and from all actions, suits, costs, charges, damages, loss and expenses whatsoever, which shall or may at any time hereafter, happen or come to them or either of them, for or by reason of the payment of the said claim by the said....................Railroad Company without having surrendered to it the said original Bill of Lading, then this obligation to be void, otherwise to remain in full force and effect.

..........................(SEAL)
..........................(SEAL)
..........................(SEAL)

* An informal bond much shorter than this form is in use by many of the best roads in the country. The shorter form omits much of the legal language contained in the longer form and simply provides that the claimant is "to indemnify the .... Railroad Company from all actions, suits, costs, charges, damages or loss or expense whatsoever which may occur by reason of the payment." on account of non-surrender of Bill of Lading.

The reasons why the carrier requires that the original bill of lading be attached to a claim are that the bill of lading is prima facie evidence of the ownership of the shipment and to that extent established the right to file a claim;[3] that it is the contract under which the shipment moves and to that extent determines the rights of the parties thereunder; and that it is also a receipt for

[3]If bill of lading is in the hands of the carriers, the papers should so state.

the shipment which it covers and is prima facie proof that the goods were delivered to the carrier. The document also contains other necessary information with regard to claims, such as the points of origin and destination, the routing, the rate on which the charge for the service is based, the nature and contents of the shipment, the weight and the amount, and the amount of the freight charge if freight charges have been prepaid. Fuller explanation of the bill of lading will be found in the treatise on that subject.

Another document which should be filed in support of a claim is (3) *the paid freight bill,* because the amount of the freight charges on a shipment upon which claim is made for total loss is an element of the damages; that is, the claimant is entitled to a return of the freight charges paid. (4) *A certified copy of the invoice* is often required on shipments moving prior to June 1, 1915, as under the third section of the uniform bill of lading in general use prior to that date, it was provided that the amount of any loss or damage for which a carrier should be liable should be computed on the basis of the value of the property at the time and place of shipment, which should be the *bona fide* invoice value thereof to the consignee, unless a lower value had been agreed upon or was determined by the tariff upon which the rate was based, in which case the lower value would be the maximum amount to be recovered. Such an invoice or copy thereof should be certified by the party rendering the same.

The Cummins Amendment to the Interstate Commerce Act, which became effective June 1, 1915, prohibited limitations of value in any form whatsoever. It was considered that the invoice value clause in the bill of lading was a limitation in violation of this amendment, and it was, therefore, eliminated so that under the present form of the uniform bill of lading it is provided in the third section thereof that "all claims for loss or damage should be based on the value of the property at the time and place of shipment." Under this provision it will be necessary to submit *an affidavit by the proper party,* which should show the value of the property lost or damaged at the time the shipment was made.

(5) *An affidavit of non-delivery of the shipment* is not absolutely necessary, for the reason that the records of the agent at destination should indicate whether or not a particular shipment has been received there. Inasmuch, however, as the object of presenting a claim is to have it allowed, it is always good policy to present claims in the strongest possible manner. In view of the fact that the records of the railroad agent are not always complete and accurate, as a matter of policy and of precaution it is suggested that an affidavit of non-receipt be attached to the claim. An affidavit of non-delivery should, of course, be made by the consignee or party in charge of shipping irrespective of whether the claim is being presented by the consignee or the consignor.

(c) Amount of Claim [4]

The amount which can be recovered for the total loss of a shipment depends upon conditions in the individual case. What is here said should be taken only as generally suggestive.

Invoice Value.—Where claim is filed to recover for the total loss of a shipment which was made under the uniform bill of lading in use *prior* to June 1, 1915, the amount of the claim should be limited to the *bona fide* invoice price to the consignee plus freight charges, if prepaid, at the time and place of shipment unless the other conditions set forth in section 3 of that form of bill of

[4] Does not apply to live stock, which is treated on page 21.

lading enter into the claim. The bill of the claimant on the carrier, therefore, would be the amount of the invoice plus the amount of the freight charges, if prepaid, and no claim on such a shipment should be filed for more than this amount.

On shipments moving *subsequent* to June 1, 1915, the amount of the claim should be the value of the property at the time and place of shipment plus whatever freight charges may have been prepaid thereon. This, as we have pointed out, is the change brought about by the Cummins Amendment to the Interstate Commerce Act.

Where a shipment consists of numerous articles of different character, the amount of the claim should be itemized, as would be the case had an invoice been rendered. Carriers are entitled to know the items comprising the total amount claimed, for the reason that it would be manifestly impossible to ascertain whether or not the amount claimed is proper in the absence of an invoice, where only a lump sum is set forth.

In cases where the amount of the claim is based upon the governing section of the uniform bill of lading (section 3), a question of construction sometimes arises as the following case will illustrate. A is a merchant to whom B, located at some other point, gives an order. A, not being able to fill the order himself, orders from C, a manufacturer located at a third point, the goods to be shipped to B. C ships to B and bills to A at manufacturer's price. A bills B at that price, with his profit. The goods are lost in transit. The question is: What is B's measure of damages under section 3 of the uniform bill of lading?

In such a case the measure of damage will still be the value of the property at the time and place of shipment. A carrier is not concerned with the manner of the sale of the property it carries, and assumes no greater liability than is set out in the contract of shipment which it issues. It has no knowledge of the parties interested in the sale and delivery of the property which it carries and for that reason is not responsible for anything except the value of the property at the time and place it receives it.

Released Valuation.—The original Cummins Amendment, which became effective June 1, 1915, expressly provides that all limitations of value or released valuations should be void and of no effect. This amendment remained in effect unchanged until August 9, 1916, when the amendment was amended so as to provide: (1) that the provisions of the original Cummins Amendment would not apply to ordinary baggage; (2) that released valuations would be valid and binding if agreed upon in writing and based on reduced rates; and (3) that such values and rates had been expressly authorized or required by order of the Interstate Commerce Commission.

The situation, therefore, is this: That on shipments moving prior to June 1, 1915, a released value is valid and binding on the shipper if based upon a reduced rate; that during the period from June 1, 1915, to August 9, 1916, no limitations of value were valid or binding and the claimant on a shipment made during that period would be entitled to recover the full value of his property, notwithstanding any declaration of value that might have been made; on shipments moving subsequent to August 9, 1916, the limitations will be valid if the provisions of the amendment of August 9 have been complied with by the carrier, that is, if the released valuations have been authorized or required by order of the Interstate Commerce Commission and agreed upon in writing by the shipper and the carrier.

It should be noted, however, that under the amendment of August 9 ordinary livestock was specifically excepted, so that on this class of freight it is still the law that all limitations of value are invalid.

With reference to claims made on shipments in intrastate transportation, it should be ascertained what the courts of the particular state in which the shipment moved have held on this question, and the amount of the claim should be fixed in accordance with the holdings, that is, whether the courts have either sustained or repudiated released valuation contracts. In a large number of the states carriers are forbidden by statute to limit by contract their common law liability, with respect to the amount which can be recovered for loss or damage to goods delivered to them for transportation; and the Supreme Courts of most of the states wherein such statutes prevail have held that a released valuation clause in the bill of lading or shipping contract is a limitation of the carriers' common law liability, and, therefore, is unlawful and non-enforcible. Briefly stated, the common law liability of a common carrier for loss or damage to shipments is that it is absolutely liable for all loss or damage suffered by a shipment after delivery to it for transportation, except loss caused by the shipper, the act of God, the public enemy, or that which is a result of the inherent vice of the thing shipped.

Conversion.—In cases where a shipment is converted by the carrier, that is, (1) where a carrier has unlawfully appropriated the property to its own use, or (2) where the carrier disposes of the shipment in a manner that amounts to conversion, the bill of lading basis, whatever it is, will govern the amount of any claim made for the value of the property. Until very recently it had been held that in such a case a claimant was entitled to the value of the property at the time and place of the conversion, but the Supreme Court of the United States has now held that even in case of a conversion the provisions of the contract of shipment, with reference to the amount to be paid, will govern and that there can be no recovery in excess of that amount. It is to be understood that this applies, however, only to interstate shipments. On intrastate shipments the local rule will govern and in most such cases the claimant is entitled to the value of the property at the time and place of the conversion.

An example of (1) is where coal is confiscated for the use of the carrier while in transit. An example of (2) is where the carrier delivers the shipment to someone not entitled to receive it, or, in other words, to anyone who is not the consignee or his agent or the holder of the bill of lading properly endorsed.

2. Partial Loss

Claims for partial loss of a shipment arise where only a part of a shipment is delivered and the carrier cannot account for the remainder.

(a) By Whom Claim May Be Presented

A claim for partial loss may be presented by (1) *the consignor* or (2) *the consignee.* The question as to who is entitled to present a claim for partial loss is fully covered under the same subheading under the general subject of "Claims for Total Loss," and need not be repeated here.

(b) Documents Filed in Support of Claim

A claim for partial loss should be supported by (1) *the bill of lading,* for the reasons heretofore given ;(2) *the paid freight bill;* (3) *the certified copy of the invoice* on shipments moving prior to June 1, 1915, or *an affidavit showing the value at time and place of shipment* on shipments moving subsequent to that date; (4) *an affidavit of loss and itemized bills for the particular part of the shipment lost* (the latter should be specific and should be made by the consignee); and (5) *the notation of loss on the freight bill.* When, upon delivery, it is ascertained that part of a shipment is missing, the party receiving the goods should insist on the presence of the carrier's agent and should demand that the notation on the freight bill state the exact amount or portions of the shipment which are missing. While the absence of such a notation is not conclusive proof that the entire shipment was delivered, its presence is exceedingly good evidence of the loss and will tend to facilitate greatly the payment of the claim by the carrier. If no such notation was secured, its absence should be explained when the claim is filed. In no case where a shipment is received, part of which is missing, should a clear receipt be given for the entire shipment. While it is also true that a clear receipt is not conclusive proof that the entire shipment was received, it is presumptive evidence of perfect delivery which must be rebutted by the claimant before the railroad claim department will allow the claim.

(c) Amount of Claim

The considerations governing the amount which the claimant is entitled to recover for a partial loss of a shipment are the same as set forth under this heading in the similar section relating to claims covering total loss; but it should be noted that it is of great importance where settlement is requested on the basis of the invoice value, or value at time and place of shipment, that the items covering the particular portions of the shipment which are missing should be specifically set forth in the affidavit of loss and itemized bill rendered. The item for return of freight charges should be based on the proportion of the freight charges covering the portion of the shipment which is missing and for which claim is filed; that is to say, if the claim is filed for partial loss of a shipment of grain, the freight charges will have been based on the weight of the shipment. Therefore, the proportion of the freight charges which the claimant is entitled to recover will be on that portion of the total freight charge which is equivalent to the charge for the weight of the grain lost.

(d) Leakage

Where claims for partial loss arise out of leakage in transit, it is necessary to present certain additional documents than those already mentioned. Owing to the difficulty of ascertaining the exact amount of loss occasioned by leakage, many of the states have enacted statutes which define strictly the duties and obligations of the carrier with respect to the class of shipments where such loss usually arises, and also the method by which claims of this character should be supported and the documents that it is necessary to present in substantiation thereof. It is impossible in this treatise to include a digest of these various statutes, as they usually differ in various details in the several states. It is therefore suggested that in preparing claims of this character the particular law governing be consulted for guidance.

Grain.—In cases of loss of grain occasioned by leakage or any other cause, where no invoice has been rendered, in order to arrive at the amount to be claimed, the general principles hereinbefore stated under that heading should be followed, and to substantiate the amount the market reports at the point of destination at the time of arrival, or, if the claim is one for both loss and delay, the time the shipment should have arrived should be submitted. If market reports are not available, then the sales reports covering the particular shipment should be submitted, properly verified. If sales reports covering the shipment cannot be had, receipts or affidavits setting forth the amount received for that portion of the shipment which was delivered when sold, should be included with the other documents filed with the claim. Claims for partial loss of grain should also be supported by an affidavit of loading weight and such affidavit should be made by the party who loaded the grain. Also a certificate of the weighmaster, if such officer exists at the point of destination, and if such a certificate cannot be procured, the affidavit of the person unloading the shipment as to the weight unloaded should be substituted. In the state of Illinois, under the statutes, it is the duty of the agent at the loading station to verify the loading weights, and in all cases this verification should be procured and noted on the bill of lading, so far as interstate shipments are concerned; however, the provisions of the Pomerene Law in Appendix D should be borne in mind

Liquids.—In addition to the documents listed and necessary to be supplied in support of claims for leakage of grain, in the case of leakage of liquids, a gauger's certificate covering the quantity loaded at the point of origin and the quantity received at the point of destination should be added. Where the shipment was not gauged by an official gauger at either point or at one or the other points, the affidavits of the parties loading and unloading should be supplied.

(e) Concealed Loss

In connection with the use of the terms "concealed loss" and "concealed damage," it would be well to state that these terms indicate that the loss or damage is of such nature that it would not be evident upon delivery by the carrier to the consignee. In the case of a consignment of shoes packed in cases, all the packages might be in apparently good order when consignee took delivery from the railroad company, but when the cases were unpacked in the consignee's plant, it would be found that a pair of shoes had been removed from each case. In another case a shipment of china might be received in apparently good order so far as the external appearance of the package was concerned, but upon opening the packages it might be found that the entire contents were broken. With this explanation, the following statements will be easily understood, as the carrier is more or less obliged to be governed by the statements of the consignee.

In view of the opportunities for fraud on the carrier in claims for concealed loss and of their natural reluctance to allow such claims unless substantiated beyond a reasonable doubt, it is of the utmost importance that claims for such loss be supported by the most complete and convincing evidence. In the very nature of the case, it is exceedingly difficult for a carrier to verify such alleged losses. Therefore, such must be supported by clear and detailed affidavits of the shipper as to the condition of the goods and packages shipped and of the contents of the various packages if the shipment consists of a number of separate articles, also by affidavits of any parties who handled the shipments after it left the shipper and before delivery to the carrier. If, from the nature of the shipment, there could have been an opportunity for pilfering or tampering while in the custody of the drayman at either end, affidavits should be secured from him and included in the claim to the effect that the packages were not tampered with while in his possession. The affidavit of the party receiving the goods should be clear and explicit as to the contents of the packages when opened and also as to the fact that there was no opportunity for tampering or pilfering during the period between the delivery by the carrier and the time when the packages were opened and when the loss was discovered.

III. CLAIMS FOR DAMAGE

Claims for loss have been considered both with respect to claims for total loss and claims for loss of any part of a shipment. Under the present heading will be considered exclusively claims for damage to a shipment, it being assumed that the entire shipment arrived at destination.

(a) By Whom Claim May Be Presented

A claim for damage may be presented by (1) *the consignor* or (2) *the consignee.* The statements governing the presentation of claims for loss by either the consignor or the consignee are also applicable to all claims that may be made for damage to a shipment; in other words, the ownership of the shipment determines by whom the claim is presented.

(b) Documents Filed in Support of Claim

A claim for damage should be supported by (1) *the original bill of lading or indemnity bond,* (2) *the paid freight bill,* and (3) *a certified copy of the invoice and an itemized bill for the damage* on shipments moving prior to June 1, 1915, or *an affidavit showing the value at time and place of shipment* on shipments moving subsequently to that date. The reasons for requiring the submission of these documents have been set out under the heading of "Claims for Loss." The reason for the submission of these documents in claims for damages are precisely the same. There should also be submitted (4) *an affidavit from the shipper* certifying to the good condition of the goods when delivered to the carrier and (5) *an affidavit from the consignee* or party who unpacks the goods, setting forth the damaged condition of the shipment when delivered to him. A notation should be made on the freight bill by the agent specifying the nature of the damage. The amount which may be billed should also be submitted in confirmation of the claim. Where the damage to the shipment is apparent at the time it is received, a careful inspection should be made of the goods by the consignee, and he should insist on the presence of the carrier's agent at the time this inspection is made. A shipment received in a damaged condition should never be receipted for as being in perfect condition; while it is not absolutely necessary that the agent make a notation on the freight bill as to the amount of damage done, still this sort of evidence, when presented by the claimant, is almost conclusive as to the damage. A receipt given by the claimant showing that the shipment was received in good condition is, of course, prima facie evidence of that fact, and where this sort of receipt has been given, it is incumbent upon the claimant to show by other proof that the shipment was not, as a matter of fact, in good condition, but was damaged to the amount claimed. It sometimes happens that the records of the carrier's agent at destination will show the amount and character of the damage where a shipment arrives in that condition; but these records are not dependable, and the consignee should, in all cases, insist that a "bad order" notation be made on the freight bill.

(c) Amount of Claim

The amount for which a claim for damage should be presented is governed by exactly the same general rules that were laid down previously under the similar heading relating to claims for total loss, the amount being dependent on whether the shipment travelled under a released valuation or under the uniform bill of lading, whether or not it was an interstate shipment, and all other points brought out in that paragraph. It should be noted, however, that the freight charges on a shipment which has been damaged do not always constitute an item of damage to which the claimant is entitled when presenting a claim. In cases where the shipment has been so damaged as to be a total loss, the freight charges which have been paid are a proper item. In claims for damage it is apparent that, if the contract of transportation has been fulfilled by the carrier, it is entitled to the freight charges which it has earned, the claimant being allowed only an amount which will compensate him for the damage done to the shipment.

(d) Claims for Damage to Livestock

A separate section is given to damage claims of this character, for the reason that a carrier's liability for such damage is somewhat different from its liability for damage to inaminate freight, and for the further reason that different documents are required in confirmation of any claim for such damage, a different degree of care being required on the part of the carrier. No bill of lading is usually issued to cover shipments of livestock. The stock travels under what is known as a livestock contract, to which the shipper and the carrier are parties, and which contains rules and regulations governing the rate to be charged, the value of the stock which is declared by the shipper, and in some instances, the care to be given the stock while in transit.

A Claim for Damage to Livestock May Be Presented by (1) *the consignor* or (2) *the consignee.* In practically every instance, claims for damage to livestock are presented by the consignor, for the reason that this sort of shipment is usually made for the purpose of sale, the sale being conducted by commission men for account of the consignor, return being made by them to him.

A Claim for Damage to Livestock Should Be Supported by (1) *the original livestock contract* or (2) *the paid freight bill.* These documents are necessary for the reasons heretofore stated, the livestock contract fulfilling the same requirements in a claim for damage to stock as are fulfilled by the bill of lading in claims on inanimate freight. There should also be submitted (3) *an affidavit by the consignor* which should cover the condition of the stock when loaded, their weight if it has been ascertained, the purpose for which the stock was intended, and the kind of stock of which the shipment consisted; (4) *an affidavit by the consignee* setting forth the condition of the stock when unloaded, showing the weight if the weight has been ascertained, and also the amount and character of the damage; (5) *a certified copy of the account of sale* covering the particular shipment on which the claim for damage is made, and also receipts or bills covering such items of damage as extra feed, etc.; and (6) *market reports* showing the prices the stock would have brought had it arrived in good condition.

In all shipments of livestock there is a certain amount of shrinkage which must be regarded as inevitable and for which no damage can properly be claimed, for the reason that it is not caused by the carrier, but results from the natural tendency of the animals to shrink during transportation. The amount of such shrinkage cannot, of course, be positively stated; but it has been variously estimated at from 2 to 3 per cent of the total weight of the shipment. It will, of course, vary under different conditions.

Amount of Claim.—The amount which a claimant is entitled to recover for damage to a shipment of livestock is also arrived at in a different manner from the amount recoverable on a claim for damage to inanimate freight. There is usually no invoice rendered, and the amount of damage is, in most cases, computed by subtracting the amount received for the stock in the condition in which it arrived and was sold from the amount which could have been realized for it at the time it should have arrived and in good condition.

In cases where livestock is *killed* in transit the measure of damage is still different. Under the law as it existed prior to June 1, 1915, the claimant in such a case was entitled to only the released value of the property where a release was executed, and such released value was based on a reduced rate published by the carrier in its tariffs on file with the Interstate Commerce Commission. As we have said, the Cummins Amendment to the Interstate Commerce Act, which became effective June 1, 1915, abolished all limitations of value so far as they pertained to livestock.

It is the present custom of the carriers to require a statement by the shipper at the time of shipment, which presumably shows the *actual* value of the stock at the time it is shipped. If in case of a total loss a shipper should claim that the value inserted in the contract was not the actual value, he would under the present law be entitled to recover in a lawsuit whatever the actual value was, but in so doing he would be contradicting his declaration of value made under the livestock contract and might be liable criminally under Section 10 of the Act to Regulate Commerce (See page 39), inasmuch as at the present time the carriers have graduated rates for the transportation of livestock based upon the actual value declared by the shipper at the time the shipment is made.

(e) Claims for Damage Caused by Delay

The scope of this section is intended to cover the damage suffered by delay as distinguished from physical damage to the shipment itself, that is, the entire amount of the damage the shipment suffers as a result of the delay, the shipment itself travelling without exception so far as physical condition is concerned. There are frequent occasions where a shipment suffers both physical damage and damage resulting from delay; for instance, grain is frequently damaged in transit by becoming wet, overheated, or mixed with other substances. Livestock frequently suffers from excessive shrinkage and physical deterioration resulting from delay, as well as from a drop in the market. In such cases claim should be made for damage covering both the physical depreciation suffered by the shipment and the damage resulting from a drop in the market where the shipment was intended for sale. The measure of damages in such cases is the difference between the amount which the shipment was worth in good condition on the date on which it should have arrived, and what was actually received for it or what could have been received for it on the date and in the condition in which it did arrive.

A Claim for Damage Due to Delay Should Be Supported by (1) *the original bill of lading* or substitute contract and (2) *the paid freight bill.* These documents are necessary for the reason heretofore given. There should also be submitted (3) *the market reports* showing the value of the commodity on the date it should have arrived, this document being necessary only in cases where the shipment was made for the purpose of sale; (4) *a report of the sale* as made showing the price actually received for the shipment; and (5) *an itemized bill* representing the difference as shown in the market reports covering the dates when the shipment should have arrived and when it did arrive. If the market reports and a report of the sale are not available, affidavits should be furnished covering the price which could have been realized had the shipment arrived on time and the price actually received therefor at the time it did arrive. The later affidavit should be made by the person to whom the goods were sold.

Amount of Claim.—The amount the claimant is entitled to recover in almost all cases where delay is the basis of the claim is the difference in the market price or value of the shipment at the time it should have arrived and the price or value it actually brought or had at the time it arrived. The only exception to this rule is a case where the goods, instead of being intended for sale, are intended for use, in which event the measure of damages is the reasonable value of the use of the article during the time of the delay.

The time which a movement should consume in order that it may not be subject to liability for delay is the reasonable time consumed in covering the distance between the points of origin and destination. Unless a carrier specifically contracts or makes time an element as a basis for particular rates and classifications contained in its published tariffs, it does not undertake to move a shipment in any particular time or the quickest possible time and is therefore liable only for failure to transport a shipment in reasonable time, which is equivalent to saying that the carrier is liable only for unreasonable and excessive delay. This subject is treated in more detail in the treatise on "Laws of Carriers of Goods."

A form to be used in filing loss or damage claims is here shown. This form may be modified to meet individual needs.

A number of firms have these forms printed in quantities for use of their claim departments, thus saving a considerable amount of clerical labor and expense.

FORM FOR LOSS OR DAMAGE CLAIM

Claim No..........
Filed ....
(Date)

..........................R. R. Co.
Dr. to
....
(Name of Claimant)

Total Amount, $............

Loss, account damage.

(Here set forth itemized statement of loss or damage.)

Papers attached:

1. Original bill of lading or shipping receipt.
2. Paid freight bill.
3. Itemized bill of claimant.
4. Original invoice or attested copy.
5. Receipted bill of the party who made repairs (if claim represents repairs).
6. Livestock claims: Original account of sales.
7. (Or whatever other document may be attached.)

....
(Signature of Claimant)

IV. OVERCHARGE CLAIMS

An overcharge claim may arise as the result of one of several things: an error in rate, that is to say, an erroneous application by the agent or shipper of the rate attributable to the particular shipment; an erroneous classification, that is, a misconception on the part of the shipper or of the agent as to which classification applies to a particular shipment; a straight overcharge on weight, which results where a greater weight than the actual weight is taken as the basis for the charge or where freight is collected on more than the amount billed.

In connection with overcharges by the carriers, we

would here suggest that it is often possible to have such overcharges adjusted without the necessity of filing a claim. Many errors in billing charges are clearly mistakes, and a little co-operation between shippers and carriers in adjusting these differences will do much to lighten the work of both. Errors in extension are quite frequent on expense bills and it is only necessary to take the matter up with the local agent to have the matter adjusted, if not before the payment of the bill, at least within a reasonable time after, by the carrier making a refund. In other cases the carrier may have billed a shipment as collect, when as a matter of fact it was prepaid at the originating point, and the submitting by the consignee of prepaid bill of lading or paid expense bill will enable the carrier to adjust the matter within a very short time. Errors sometimes arise entirely from the application of an erroneous rate which is immediately evident and will be adjusted simply by calling the carrier's attention to the matter. Adjustment of overcharges in the manner above suggested generally means a considerable saving of time and expense, as the natural routine of a claim is such that some additional time is consumed in handling even the simplest matter.

The subjects of tariffs, classifications, routing, etc., are not within the scope of this treatise, and reference should be had to the other treatises in this course covering these subjects. The legal basis of an overcharge claim rests in the fact that there can be only one lawful charge for any particular shipment as billed, classified, and routed. Therefore, the problem is to ascertain what tariff and classifications govern the shipment in question. These being ascertained, it is a simple matter to compute the correct charge. If the amount paid differs one way or the other, it is the duty of the carriers either to refund if the result is an overcharge or to collect the difference if the result is an undercharge. To establish his claim for an overcharge the claimant has only to show by the means hereinbefore set forth that the amount paid was more than the amount lawfully due under the carriers' tariffs. Inasmuch as the rates charged by the carriers for particular services are under the constant scrutiny of the Interstate Commerce Commission for the purpose of enabling that body to ascertain whether or not the carriers are making unlawful discriminations, there will be no difficulty in the collection of overcharge claims when properly presented and substantiated. The published tariffs of the carriers constitute the sole basis upon which it is permitted to charge for services rendered. Therefore, it is of particular importance in the presentation of overcharge claims that the tariff authority relied upon in substantiation of claims be clearly and accurately stated. It should also be kept in mind that no claim against a carrier for damage resulting from a *misquotation* of rate can be collected. The U. S. Supreme Court has held that shippers are presumed under the law to know what the published tariffs contain.

On the question of overcharge in weight, however, complications sometimes arise. On carload shipments of lumber and coal, for example, the marked tare weight of the car is almost entirely used in arriving at the net weight of the shipment, upon which the charges are assessed, and this tare weight of the car is very frequently erroneous. Also, charges on weights are very often assessed in accordance with the marked minimum weight of a shipment which a car will hold, this method of arriving at a rate being provided for in most cases by tariff, but very often, as a matter of fact, the car will not hold as much as the stated weight, which will result in an overcharge. A shipment should always be weighed at point of origin and the actual weight inserted on the bill of lading, together with a notation signed by the agent of the carrier that the car is loaded to full visible capacity, as these are the only circumstances under which such claims will ever be allowed. In shipments of lumber, especially, estimated weights are largely used in arriving at the total weight of a shipment, as the weight of lumber, when shipped, depends a great deal on the way in which it is cut, on its condition (whether dry or wet), and other things. It is very desirable in shipments of this kind that the shipments be weighed as many times as possible in transit so that a correct average weight can be arrived at. In presenting claims a record of the various weighings should be included if possible.

(a) By Whom Claim May Be Presented

A claim for an overcharge may be presented by (1) *the consignor* or (2) *the consignee,* depending on which pays the freight charges. Claims for overcharge should be presented by whoever paid the freight, whether it be the consignor or the consignee.

(b) Documents Filed in Support of Claim

A claim for an overcharge should be supported by (1) *the original bill of lading* or, if the original bill of lading is not available, the shipping receipt or an indemnity bond in the event of the claimant's inability to furnish either one or the other documents; (2) *the paid freight bill,* which is an absolutely necessary document, as it is evidence of the amount of freight paid; (3) *a citation to the tariff authority* in support of the claim if the overcharge claim is based on an error in rate or classification; and (4) *the original invoice* for the purpose of showing weights, or an affidavit of the shipper if the claim is for an overcharge in weight. A bill of lading is not an absolutely necessary document on an overcharge claim, as practically the only purpose which it serves is to show the date of shipment, and by that, the rate in effect at the time the shipment moved.

A form to be used in filing overcharge claims is here shown. This form may be modified to meet individual needs.

FORM FOR CLAIM FOR OVERCHARGE

.... Claim No..........
(Name of Claimant)

Pro. No............

Against...............................R. R. Co.

Date of Claim................

No. of Car................. Shipped by................
Initials of Car............. From ....
No. of Waybill.............. Shipped to ....
Date of Waybill............ At. ....
Weight charged......Rate charged......Amount charged....
Weight should be...Rate should be....Amount should be.....
Amount of Claim............

Papers attached:

1. Original bill of lading.
2. Paid freight bill.
3. Itemized bill of claimant.
4. Original invoice, or attested copy, minus prices. (If overcharge in weight.)
5. Reference to tariff number authorizing claimed rate. (If overcharge in rate.)

....
(Signature of Claimant)

V. GENERAL SUGGESTIONS

1. Claim Department Methods of Handling Claims

Upon receipt of a claim in a railroad claim department office, it is first handled by a clerk who attaches a fileback to the papers, classifies it, gives it a file number, acknowledges receipt, and examines the papers submitted for the purpose of ascertaining whether or not the various documents which the carrier requires in substantiation of the claim are present. If any of the documents which have been enumerated in the foregoing sections of this treatise are absent, it frequently happens that the claim will be declined on that ground. Such a declination, however, should not be accepted, but the missing documents should be supplied and the claim again urged upon the attention of the department. The fact that the claim department sometimes takes advantage of the failure of the claimant to present all documents required in substantiation of the claim illustrates the very great importance of using care in the preparation of claims and of seeing to it that the various documents which have hereinbefore been set forth are included in the first instance. A delay of at least two weeks will thus be avoided and extra work on the part of all saved.

If an acknowledgment of the receipt of the claim is not received within a comparatively short time, a letter should be dispatched requesting information as to whether or not the claim was received and insisting upon acknowledgment.

After the above preliminaries have been attended to, the claim will, in due course, come before some one higher in the department whose duty it is to start the investigation of the claim. Many claimants are under the impression that the carriers should pay a claim submitted in proper form and properly substantiated immediately upon receipt. The claimant knows that he has a valid claim and finds it difficult to understand why the carrier will not immediately acknowledge and pay it when completely and properly presented. Whatever the reasons may have been in the past, the reason now is that carriers are compelled by law to investigate thoroughly claims before paying the same. It is apparent that if the rule were otherwise, there would be innumerable opportunities for discrimination in favor of certain shippers under the device of payment of claims. Only recently a number of prominent eastern roads were very heavily fined for precisely this practice. Inasmuch as carriers are compelled to keep all of their accounts in accordance with the methods prescribed by the Interstate Commerce Commission, and inasmuch as the records and accounts of the carriers are always open to the inspection of the investigators of the Commission, and inasmuch as the Commission, as a matter of fact, exercises a very close and careful scrutiny on the revenues and disbursements of the carriers, it is easy to understand why the carrier refuses to pay claims, however just they may appear, without a thorough and complete investigation.

As the carriers' methods of handling freight claims are fully explained in *The Investigation of Freight Claims,* the subject will not be given further consideration here. The reader will do well to make a study of the above-mentioned treatise, as it will assist him in handling claims more proficiently.

In view of the fact that certain of the documents such as paid freight bills and bills of lading cannot be replaced except by certified copies in the event that the original set is lost, it is important that claim papers be securely fastened together by some device other than pins before papers are submitted to the carriers.

2. Details

Since, during the course of an investigation claim papers go through many hands and are frequently sent to the claim departments of other roads, there is danger of their becoming lost or misplaced. All documents filed with the claim should, therefore, always be prepared in duplicate and a complete set retained by the claimant for his own convenience for purposes of reference and to enable him to supply the carrier with a duplicate set in case the originals become lost.

When a claim is declined the claimant is entitled to a return of all the original papers submitted.

In all correspondence with claim departments it is important to quote accurately the railroad claim number. Much delay will be saved if this is done, as reference to the claim by number under the system universally used in railroad claim offices is much more easy and expeditious than by any other method.

3. Promptness in Filing Claims

Bills of lading and shipping contracts usually specifically provide the time within which claims may be filed. On shipments moving prior to June 1, 1915, the date of the original Cummins Amendment to the Interstate Commerce Act, these stipulations in contracts of shipment as to the time in which claims should be presented were valid and enforcible, and a failure by the claimant to present his claim within the time allowed would be a valid defense to the claim. The Cummins Amendment referred to provides that there shall be no shorter period for giving notice of claim than ninety days, but further provides that if the loss, damage, or injury complained of was due to delay or damage while being loaded or unloaded or damage in transit by carelessness or negligence, then no notice of claim or filing of claim shall be required as a condition precedent to recovery. It will be noted that on shipments moving after this amendment became effective, the carrier would have to have a perfect defense on the merits in order to take advantage of the time limit for filing claims. In other words, there is no obligation upon a shipper to file a claim within the time allowed if the loss or damage complained of arises from any of the causes mentioned, and inasmuch as such causes include practically all causes which would operate to make a carrier liable for the loss, this provision is practically of no effect, and it is suggested that failure to file within the time allowed be not accepted by the claimant as a ground for declination of a claim by the carrier. Nevertheless, it is advisable, as a matter of policy, to present claims as promptly as possible.

With reference to the time for filing claims, a distinction must be noted between claims arising out of interstate and intrastate shipments. With respect to the latter, the courts of most states have held that clauses in bills of lading and shipping contracts requiring claims to be filed within a definite period, or disclaiming liability if not so filed, are limitations of the common law liability of the carrier and, therefore, unlawful and nonenforcible.

4. Special Damages

Much confusion exists in the minds of many claimants as to just what damages can be recovered where shipments have been lost or damaged. Most of what is important in this connection has already been covered under the subhead "Amount of Claim" under the various classes of claims treated in this treatise; but for the general information of the student it is deemed advisable to explain, in a general way, the distinction between the elements of damage which can be recovered from a carrier and those which are called "special damages" and which are not recoverable. Special damages are defined as damages not within the contemplation of the parties when the contract covering the shipment was made. In order to hold a carrier liable for special damages, it is necessary that an agent of the carrier be informed at the time the contract is made of any special circumstances in connection with the shipment which will result in special loss to the shipper in the event of loss or damage to the shipment, either through physical damage or delay. In the absence of such notice, the carrier cannot be held liable for special damages. It is important to note that such notice must be given the carrier at the time the contract of shipment is entered into, as subsequent notice will not render the carrier liable for the reason that such notice given after the contract of transportation has been consummated between the carrier and the shipper is held to be an additional obligation imposed upon the carrier which is not in the contemplation of the parties at the time the original contract is made. This is true even though the notice be given subsequent to the entering into of the contract but before the occurrence which causes the special damage.

To explain clearly what is meant by special damages the following examples are recited. A shipper of grain has an opportunity to sell grain in another town at an advance of ten cents over the published market price if it is delivered on a certain date. He makes the shipment without informing the carrier of the special circumstances. The car is delayed and the shipper loses his ten cent profit by reason thereof, although there has been no decline in the published market price. A claim filed by him for the ten-cent loss will not be allowed. Or, again, a manufacturer of machinery in Chicago ships to St. Louis, Mo., a consignment of machinery. Let us suppose the schedule time for shipments of this character between the two points is 24 hours. The machinery is such that it requires the services of an expert from the manufacturing plant to install it, and the shipper, figuring on the arrival of the shipment on schedule time, sends a man to St. Louis for the purpose of installing the machinery. The shipment is delayed for three days, and, as a result, the shipper is put to the expense of maintaining his expert for the extra time. Assuming that no notice was given to the carrier that such damage would accrue if the shipment did not arrive on schedule time, the answer is that such damages are special, the carrier not having had notice that such damage would accrue in the event of its failure to deliver on time. It could not have had the contingency in mind when the contract was made, and, therefore, is not liable for the loss.

In this, and similar cases, the possibility of collecting special damages would often be enhanced by written notice at the time the contract of shipment is made. Such notices should be very specific so that there will be no question as to their meaning. At best special damages are generally difficult of collection.

5. Refused Shipments

It should be noted in presenting claims for delay on the part of the carrier or carriers over whose lines a shipment travels, that no matter how excessive such delay may be, the consignee is not justified in refusing a shipment when it finally does arrive at its destination where the basis for such a refusal to accept is delay solely. There are times when a shipment arrives at destination in such condition as to be absolutely worthless, in which case the consignee is justified in refusing to accept it and in filing a claim, basing the amount on the invoice value plus all freight charges which have been paid. Mere delay, however, where no damage is done to a shipment, or where the shipment is not so damaged as to be worthless, is not sufficient ground for a refusal of the shipment, and, in all such cases, it is the duty of the consignee to accept the shipment or to give disposition orders and then to place claim with the carriers for whatever amount of damage he has suffered. Demurrage, however, which accrues during the time the shipper or consignee delays in accepting the shipment or otherwise disposing of it, cannot be included in a claim for damage or delay.

6. To Which Carrier Claims Should Be Presented

As a general rule, claims should be presented to the bill of lading carrier, that is to say, the carrier with whom the original contract of transportation is made. In cases, however, where a shipment has been handled by more than one carrier, the claim may be presented to the initial carrier, the delivering carrier, or any intermediate carrier. For the purpose of avoiding delay, however, it is always advisable, where it is convenient, to file claims with either the initial or the delivering carrier, for between the carriers where the responsibility for loss or damage cannot be located, settlement is effected on the basis of the proportionate share of the earnings on the shipment. Claims based on shipments which have travelled over more than one line are quite likely to suffer great delay on account of disputes between the carriers as to which is responsible for the damage or in an attempt by the carriers involved to place the responsibility definitely upon one or the other. When it becomes apparent to the claimant that the claim is being delayed on this account, where otherwise proper for payment, the claimant should insist upon immediate settlement by the carrier to whom the claim was presented. Practically all of the carriers have subscribed to rules and agreements covering the distribution of the amounts paid on claims where the responsibility cannot be located. The carrier with which the claim has been filed has its remedy as against the other carriers if it is entitled to reimbursement, and failure upon its part to effect a settlement with the other carriers does not justify or excuse a refusal to pay the claim.

7. Affidavits

Affidavits should always be made by a person who is conversant with the facts set forth in the affidavit. An affidavit based on information and belief is practically worthless and will probably be treated as such by the carrier. Affidavits should not contain conclusions, but should consist solely of statements of fact.

FORM OF AFFIDAVIT COVERING CONCEALED LOSS

State of .... }
County of .... } ss.

.............................., being duly sworn, on oath, deposes and says that he is (insert position) of the (insert name of claimant); that he has entire charge of all shipments coming into the place of business of said (insert name of claimant); that on the...........day of......................, A. D. 19...., he received from the........................Railroad Company a case of shoes shipped by........................ from.........................., on the...........day of ...., A. D. 19....; that he opened the said case immediately upon receiving it and checked out....... pairs of shoes.

....

Subscribed and sworn to before me this.......day of................, A. D. 19....

....

(Seal) Notary Public

Great care should be used in seeing to it that statements made in affidavits are true. It is provided in Section 10 of the Federal Interstate Commerce Act that "* * * any person, corporation or company, or any agent or officer thereof, * * * who shall knowingly and wilfully, directly or indirectly, himself or by employee, agent, officer, or otherwise, by false statement or representation as to cost, value, nature or extent of injury, or by the use of any false bill, bill of lading, receipt, voucher, roll, account, claim, certificate, affidavit, or deposition knowing the same to be false, fictitious, or fraudulent, or to contain any false, fictitious, or fraudulent statement of entry, obtain or attempt to obtain any allowance, refund, or payment for damage or otherwise in connection with or growing out of the transportation of or agreement to transport such property, whether with or without the consent or connivance of the carrier, whereby the compensation of such carrier for such transportation, either before or after payment, shall in effect be made less than the regular rates then established and in force on the line of transportation, shall be deemed guilty of fraud which is hereby declared to be a misdemeanor and shall, upon conviction thereof, in any court of the United States of competent jurisdiction, within the district in which such offense was wholly or in part committed, be subject for each offense to a fine of not exceeding Five Thousand Dollars, or imprisonment in the penitentiary for a term of not exceeding two years, or both, in the discretion of the court: *Provided,* that the penalty of imprisonment shall not apply to artificial persons."

For the benefit of the industrial man, we would suggest that it is often possible to secure prompt handling of claims through the co-operation of the traffic department of the railroad. The solicitor or commercial agent of the carrier will generally be very glad to take up with his claim department any particular claim in which the shipper may be interested. In this way, it is often possible to have claims taken care of more promptly than would be the case if the claims were left to follow the regular course of events. It should not be understood in connection with this, however, that the traffic department can or will do anything more than to secure prompt handling of claims, for, as previously stated in this treatise, the carriers are required by law to make a thorough investigation before paying a claim and should not under any circumstances pay claims until they have made such thorough investigation.

8. The Freight Claim Association

It has been stated in the "Foreword" of this treatise that at the present time carriers on the whole are making an honest and efficient endeavor to handle claims expeditiously and with a view toward bringing about a fair adjustment of the rights of the parties. It may be of interest to the reader to know something about an organization known as the Freight Claim Association, the object of which is as stated in its constitution, " * * * the prompt settlement of freight claims with claimants and between carriers." This organization is composed for the most part of the freight claim agents of practically all of the carriers of the country. It has adopted a constitution and rules which prescribe in detail the method of dealing as between the carriers with reference to loss, damage, and overcharge claims. These rules cover practically every conceivable question which may arise in the course of the dealings of the carriers with each other on claims involving shipments which have passed over the lines of more than one carrier.

Many of the rules of the Freight Claim Association with reference to the claims included within the scope of this treatise have been stated in a general way in the body of the treatise. Specific reference is made here to the Freight Claim Association not so much with the object of attempting to set forth the gist of its rules as to acquaint the student with the fact that such an organization exists and that its object is to promote prompt settlement of claims and facilitate all the various processes which must be followed before a claim can be properly investigated and passed upon. Freight claim agents in their correspondence with claimants frequently, in explanation of their course with reference to a decision upon some point having to do with a claim, refer to the rules of the Freight Claim Association, and in order that the student may understand what is meant by such reference, and for the further purpose of enabling the student to get a more adequate conception of the methods used by carriers in handling claims, this subject is inserted in the treatise.

9. Conclusion

Too great emphasis cannot be laid upon the paramount importance of presenting a claim in the strongest possible shape. While it may not be absolutely necessary to include all of the documents which have been set forth and explained under the various classes of claims hereinbefore enumerated, it is eminently desirable that they all be submitted. As has been explained, payment of claims cannot be expected within a very short period of time. It should be the object of the claimant to assist the carrier as much as possible and thus to facilitate the passage of his claim to payment by giving all possible information with regard to it and by leaving nothing undone on his part to convince the carrier that he is entitled to redress. It must be borne in mind that from one point of view amounts paid out by the carriers on claims are a dead loss and it is too much to expect that the carrier will take an active interest in promoting a claim. The claimant in his statement of the basis for his claim should, therefore, leave no loophole through which the carrier might properly escape liability.

While no attempt is made in this treatise to enter into questions of law or pass upon the merits of claims, it is not out of place to call attention to certain matters which have an important bearing upon the determining of the validity and amount of claims. In making these suggestions it is only intended to indicate matters that may have to be given consideration in the various cases.

(a) Cummins Amendment

In Appendix C the Cummins Amendment will be found reproduced in full. This amendment as originally passed was a source of much discussion on the part of traffic men, because it apparently forbade the carriers to limit their liability in the transportation of property, including not only freight but express and baggage. Owing to the unsatisfactory conditions produced by this amendment, it was amended effective August 9, 1916, to remove the principal sources of criticism. As the amendment now stands, its most important provision is to forbid the limitation of liability on livestock. It should also be noted that the last part of the amendment specifically recognizes the right of the carriers to limit the time for filing claims and starting suits. (See, however, page 33.)

As is the case with most new legislation, there are points that are not subject to the same interpretation by everyone.

(b) Pomerene Bill of Lading Law

For a great many years a serious source of controversy has arisen through doubts as to just how far the carrier can be held liable for property for which a bill of lading had been signed. The United States Supreme Court has held that the carrier might not be held liable for property for which the bill of lading had been signed but which had actually not been received by the carrier. In a general way it may be stated that the court based this holding upon the ground that a representative of the carrier was going beyond his authority in receipting for property which he had not actually received. This meant that a considerable number of frauds were perpetrated upon the banks and others through the use of fraudulent bills of lading, with the result that the order bill of lading was not accepted in many cases because of fear of loss through some fraud. To remove this source of difficulty as well as to provide uniform regulations in connection with bills of lading, the Pomerene Bill of Lading Law was passed by Congress and became effective January 1, 1917. This law is reproduced in full in Appendix D. No attempt is here made to analyze this bill or to interpret its various provisions. It will be well, however, to make a careful reading of the various provisions of the law. Some of these sections are of importance in a strictly legal sense, while other sections, such as sections 8 and 21, are of direct practical interest to traffic men in general. It should be understood that the Pomerene Law does not affect the conditions appearing upon bills of lading except as specifically mentioned in the law. It does not, for example, deal with the matter of the limitation of time for filing claims.

TEST QUESTIONS

These questions are for the student to use in testing his knowledge of the assignment. The answers are not to be sent to the University.

1. State briefly what the treatise is about.

2. Distinguish a claim for loss from a claim for damage, and a claim for overcharge.

3. How does a claim for total loss arise? Give two examples.

4. By whom may a claim for loss be presented, and what determines? State the general rule.

5. Enumerate the documents necessary to be filed with a claim for (a) total loss, (b) partial loss. State with reference to each why it is required.

6. Is an affidavit of non-delivery necessary with claims for loss? State reason for your answer.

7. Are freight charges a proper item in a claim for (a) total loss, (b) partial loss? State the reason in each case.

8. How is the amount of a claim for total loss determined where an invoice has been rendered and the shipment moved under the uniform bill of lading?

9. What is meant by the term "released valuation," and how does a "released valuation" affect the amount for which a claim for loss should be filed?

10. Is there any difference in the effect of a "released valuation" as to interstate and intrastate shipments? If so, what and why?

11. What is meant by the term "conversion"?

12. What considerations govern the amount of the claim on a "converted" shipment? State the basis of the measure of damages on such claims suggested in the treatise.

13. Is a "clear receipt" conclusive that a shipment was received without having suffered partial loss?

14. What additional burden rests upon a claimant who files a claim for partial loss, where the carrier holds a "clear receipt" for the shipment?

15. What documents in addition to those already enumerated in your answer to question 5 should be submitted with claims for partial loss of (a) grain, (b) liquids? Why?

16. Why are carriers reluctant to recognize claims for concealed loss and damage? What affidavits should be filed with such claims?

17. Are freight charges ever a proper item in a claim for damage? If so, when and why?

18. By whom are claims for loss and damage to livestock usually presented and why?

19. What constitutes extra shrinkage? Is a carrier liable for it?

20. How is the amount of a livestock claim computed where the claim is based on (a) loss and damage, (b) delay?

21. Is it proper to file a claim based on both damage and delay to the same shipment? If so, state the method of arriving at the amount of the claim and give an illustration.

22. What constitutes delay to a shipment?

23. What is an overcharge? How may an overcharge arise? Give two illustrations.

24. Is there any particular reason for filing an original bill of lading with an overcharge claim? If so, what is it?

25. Why is it important to file claims promptly? When should a livestock claim be filed and why?

26. Explain what is meant by the term "special damages." Are such damages recoverable? Can you think of illustrations other than those contained in the treatise?

27. Can consignee recover on a claim based on the value of a shipment which has been delayed in transit, assuming that the shipment itself suffered no damage? State the proper procedure in such cases.

28. Where a shipment was routed over the lines of several different carriers, to which of the carriers should a claim for loss, damage, or overcharge be presented?

29. By whom should affidavits be made and what should they contain?

APPENDIX A

For the benefit of readers who may not have had experience in the actual handling of claims, we give on the following pages copies of some of the documents and correspondence appearing in a claim relative to fruit which was received at destination in a damaged condition.

The various reports shown in this claim would vary with the nature and condition of the individual claim. Besides the correspondence shown in this appendix, there would be numerous other letters and memorandums which have not been shown, as they would not be of any particular value to show just how carriers handle their claims. In connection with the reports shown, it might be well to state that some of the words, figures, and marks are of significance only to the particular carrier using the particular form, and it is not necessary for the reader to try to understand them. The significant facts bearing on this claim are all plainly shown.

It should be borne in mind that the reader in actually handling claims would find that every claim presents its own problem to solve. The forms and methods used by various carriers are different, but they all work with the same result in mind, that is, to ascertain what are the exact facts in the individual case and to adjust the claim on that basis.

DOCUMENT 1

LETTER OF CLAIMANT TRANSMITTING CLAIM

February 10, 1913.

F. G. A., C. & G. N. R. R.,
Chicago, Ill.

Fort Valley Comm. Co. *vs.* C. & G. N. Ry. Co.

DEAR SIR:

Herewith enclosed please find statement of claim in favor of the above shippers for loss and damage to X. Y. Z. car 3031, green fruit, out of Winters, Calif., June 22, 1912, to Oelwein, Ia., account over-heated in transit. We attach in support of above claim

1. Copy of original expense bill of your company dated August 2, 1913.
2. Inspector's report signed by A. B. Smith.
3. Certified copy of original invoice showing f. o. b. cost at shipping point.
4. Copy of account sales showing gross amount realized.

We will secure original bill of lading in support of the above claim and forward same to you in the near future. Kindly acknowledge receipt of these inclosures, quote claim number of your office and company to cover, and hurry this little claim to early investigation and settlement, thereby obliging

Yours very truly.
FORT VALLEY COMM. CO.

Document 2

STATEMENT OF CLAIM

Feb. 1, 1913.

C. & G. N. R. R.

To Fort Valley Commission Co., Dr.

Our Claim No. 147.

To Loss and Damage on car No. 3031, X. Y. Z. Shipped Winters, Calif., 6/22/12. Destination Oelwein, Ia. Please adjust promptly.

Papers Attached:

1. Original Paid Expense Bill.
2. Certified Copy of Original Invoice.
3. Statement of Sales.
4. Inspector's Report.

To John Jones, General Agent.

To loss car green fruit arrived over-heated, ice plug in the bunker and fruit more or less decayed and showing heavy shrinkage.

20 crates apricots dumped account worthless	$ 29.00
80 crates peaches dumped account worthless	$ 96.00
90 crates apricots sold for $67.50 cost $130.50	$ 63.00
Loss 20 cents crate on 70 crates peaches	$ 14.00
Expense selling	$ 13.75
Extra labor	$ 14.25
Total claim	$230.00

Document 3

A CERTIFIED COPY OF ORIGINAL INVOICE

Document 4

INSPECTOR'S REPORT

This report shows that the inspector, A. B. Smith, found doors of car closed, ice plug in tank closed, temperature inside of car 62°, bunkers about half full, and that peaches and apricots were over-ripe and showed shrinkage.

Document 5

FREIGHT BILL

The paid freight bill here attached had a notation on it that freight checked 20 boxes of apricots and 80 boxes of peaches badly moulded.

Document 6

COPY OUT REPORT

This report contains an itemized statement showing just how much was realized from the sale of each kind of fruit and showing 20 boxes of apricots and 80 boxes of peaches dumped.

Document 7[1]

NOTICE OF DAMAGE TO FREIGHT

The following form illustrates how some claimants protect themselves against carriers' declining their claim on account of claim not being filed in sufficient time. Such a form is of special use in connection with the clause on the Uniform Bill of Lading, specifying the time in which the claim must be filed. The reader will notice that the claim is made for a specified amount, subject to change later on.

Oelwein, Iowa, 8/15/12

M. J. Edwards...........Local Freight Agent.
..........*C. & G. N.* ....Railroad Company
..............*Oelwein, Iowa*........................
(Destination)

DEAR SIR:

You are hereby notified that a consignment of......*Gr. Fruits*.... consisting of about.....................arrived at your station on or about......*July 2, 1912*.......over the line of said....*C. & G. N.*..... Railroad in .....*X. Y. Z.*...... car number ....*3031*..... in a badly damaged condition, caused by the negligence of said....*C. & G. N.*..... .... Railroad Company and connecting carriers.

[1] In this and the following reports shown in this appendix, the information furnished by the person making out the report is shown in italics.

As owners of said merchandise, or as representatives of such owners, we hereby make claim and demand upon said ....*C. & G. N.*........ Railroad Company, and all interested connecting carriers, for the sum of ....*$250.00*......damages by reason of the premises. If, on final disposition of this consignment, the loss shall prove MORE OR LESS than......*$250.00*,......we will so advise you and AMEND CLAIM ACCORDINGLY. Please acknowledge receipt hereof, handing us claim number for future reference.

Yours truly,

Fort Valley Commission Co.

By.........................

Document 8

Letter of local agent at Oelwein, transmitting the foregoing notice to the Freight Claim Agent at Chicago, together with a copy of his O. S. & D. (over, short, and damage) report.

Document 9

A circular letter to the agent of the C. & G. N. R. R. at Council Bluffs and Oelwein, from the Freight Claim Agent, requesting information on the following matters: (1) Date and time of arrival and departure of the car; (2) amount of ice in bunkers; (3) amount of ice added, if any; (4) condition of the drip pipes and ventilators; and (5) result of the inspection of contents of car.

Document 10

Report of agent at Council Bluffs. Car received from Union Pacific, June 28, 9:30 A. M.; sealed both sides, S. P. Co. 19 W; forwarded same date in extra at 9:25 P. M.; sealed S. P. Co. 19 W and 89636; bunkers ¾ full when received and forwarded, no ice added; vents closed, drip pipes flowing freely; contents apparently O. K.

Document 11

Report of agent at Oelwein. Car arrived June 29, 2 P. M.; delivered July 1, 7 A. M.; bunkers ⅔ full ice.

Document 12

Freight Claim Agent's request of Division Superintendent for movement of the car over the line of the C. & G. N. R. R.

Document 13

MOVEMENT REPORT

The movement report requested on Document 12 showed arriving time and leaving time at Council Bluffs and Clarion, arriving time at Oelwein, and train numbers and conductors' names.

Document 14

Letter dated March 3, 1913, by F. C. A. of the C. & G. N. R. R. to the Asst. Gen. Mgr. of the Union Pacific at Omaha, requesting the following information: (1) Complete and detailed car movement; (2) schedule; (3) record of maximum and minimum temperature at every station where taken; (4) complete icing record; and (5) position and condition of ventilators and ice plugs.

Document 15

INFORMATION ASKED FOR IN DOCUMENT 14

Union Pacific Railroad Company

C. & G. N. Claim No. *A-9022-2*
Amount of Claim *$230.00* *Omaha, Neb., 3-18-1913*
Mr. *J. Gray*, F. C. A., C. & G. N. R. R., File 8.
Chicago, Ill.

As requested by you under date of *3/3/13*, below please find our record of
(Initial) (Number)
Car X. Y. Z 3031 Capacity of Tanks *11000 lbs.* Contents *Gr. Fruit*
From *Winters, Cal.* To *Omaha, Neb.* Final Destination, *Oelwein, Iowa.*

(This document is continued on next page.)

DOCUMENT 15—*Continued*

RECEIVED AT *Ogden* From	ICE In Tanks When Received	ICE Furnished (Pounds)	SALT Furnished (Pounds)	WASTE PIPES Open or Rec'd	WASTE PIPES Closed For'd	HATCH COVERS When Rec'd (Open or closed) Seals	HATCH COVERS Forwarded (Open or closed) Seals
So. Pac. Date *6/25/12* Time *11:15 A. M.* Temp. Max. *100* " Min. *60* " When Insp. *82* Weather Conditions *Clear*				*Open*	*Open*	*Closed* *No Seals*	*Closed*
Evanston Date *6/25* Time *8:15 P. M.* Temp. Max. *78* " Min. *43* " When Insp. *59* Weather Conditions *Rain*		*2750*		*1 Open*	*1 Open*	*Closed*	*1 Closed*
No. Platte Date *6/27* Time *3:40 P. M.*		*3440*		*1 Open*	*1 Open*	*Closed*	*1 Closed*
Co. Bluffs Date *6/28* Time *5:50 A. M.* Temp. Max. *100* " Min. *71* " When Insp. *71* Weather Conditions *Clear*				*1 Open*	*1 Open*	*Closed*	*1 Closed*

Waybill Instructions *Reice at all regular icing stations.*
Remarks: *Cannot cut out at Omaha—Handled through to Co. Bluffs.*

DOCUMENT 16

Letter of F. C. A. of the C. & G. N. R. R. to the Supt. of Transp. of the So. Pac., dated March 3, 1913, reqesting same information as in Document 14.

DOCUMENT 17

Report dated March 24, 1913, of the Supt. of Transp. of the So. Pac., containing similar information to that as shown in Document 15 as follows:

SUMMARY OF INVESTIGATION OF PERISHABLE FREIGHT CLAIM

3/8-1913

Car { **Initials** *X. Y. Z.* / **Number** *3031* }   Claim *A-9022-2*

Claimant *Fort Valley Com. Co.*

Contents ....
From *Winters, Cal.*
Date *6-22-12*   Waybill *SP 75*   *$230.00*
Destined *Via Ogden*   Diverted to.........Rediverted to.........
Route ....
Instructions ....
Basis of Claim ....

MOVEMENT	DATE	HOUR	Station Temperature	Government Temperature	Ice Bunkers on Arrival	Ice Added	Positions of Ventilators	SEALS Sides	SEALS Vents	REMARKS
Car ordered	*6/20/12*									
Car placed	*6/21/12*	*3:00 P. M.*								
Loading commenced										
Loading finished	*6/22/12*									
Car released										
Car forwarded	*6/22/12*	*3:00 P. M.*	*90*			*11000*				
Roseville	*6/23/12*	*10:30 P. M.*	*88*							
		11:00 A. M.	*79*			*2000*		*19W*		
Truckee	*6/24/13*	*11:30 P. M.*	*66*							
		12:30 A. M.	*56*			*1000*				
		2:15 A. M.	*32*							
Sparks		*3:00 A. M.*	*80*							
		8:25 P. M.	*39*							
Carlin		*9:45 P. M.*	*72*			*1000*				
		11:15 A. M.	*38*							
Ogden	*6/25/13*	*1:05 P. M.*	*100*							
			60					*19W*	*28R*	
Time in transit			*68:15*							
Schedule			*61:40*							
Delay			*6:35*							

DOCUMENT 18.

Letter of claimant dated April 7, 1913, enclosing the bill of lading, which was omitted when claim was submitted.

DOCUMENTS 19 AND 20

Letter of F. C. A. of the C. & G. N. R. R. to the agent of the S. P. at Winters, Cal., requesting detailed information as to the condition of the shipment when loaded and the agent's reply thereto. Fruit in good shipping condition, fully iced, properly braced, and stored in car.

DOCUMENT 21

Additional letters of the F. C. A. of the C. & G. N. R. R., requesting explanation of discrepancies in reports previously received as follows:

Chicago, April 17, 1913.
C. & G. N. Claim No.
Fort Valley Com. Co.
$230.00

Mr. F. Smith, Supt.
Clarion, Ia.

I am referring to you the papers in this claim and call your attention to the outline statement showing the handling of the car over all rails.

This car seems to have been last iced at North Platte, Neb., on June 27. Was the car iced at Clarion, Ia.? According to agent at Co. Bluffs, the bunkers were 3/4 full when handled at his station. It does not seem that we have a complete icing record from North Platte, Neb., to Oelwein, because the car could not have arrived at Oelwein with bunkers 2/3 full unless iced between North Platte and the destination. Was there any delay on the Western Division? What was the position of the ventilators, ice plugs, and hatches? Were waste pipes open and flowing freely?

Please complete the investigation on the Western Division and return the papers promptly.

Signed ....
Freight Claim Agent.

Chicago, April 17, 1913.
C. & G. N. Claim No.
Fort Valley Com. Co.
$230.00

Agent,
Oelwein, Ia.

X. Y. Z. Car 3031 loaded with green fruit arrived in your yards at 11:35 A. M. on June 29, 1912. Your O. S. & D. Report No. 504 of July 3, 1912, states that delivery was made on that date. Shipment checking out 20 boxes apricots and 80 boxes peaches over-ripe and mouldy, while the original O. S. & D. No. 491, dated July 3, 1912, does not carry any notations as to damage.

Furthermore, in reply to mine of August 23 you advised that car arrived at 2 P. M. on June 29 and was delivered July 1, 7 A. M. I want you to go into this matter carefully, advising as to the exact time of arrival, quantity of ice in the bunkers at that time, and position of ice plugs and hatches. Were the waste pipes open and flowing freely? At what hour and on what date was delivery made to the consignee? On what date did you check the consignment? What was the exact extent of the damage and what in your opinion caused the damage? Shipment is covered by Winters, Cal., W/B SP 75, June 22, 1912.

Signed ....
Freight Claim Agent.

Document 22

STATEMENT OF CLAIM SHOWING METHOD OF CARRIER SUMMARIZING THE FACTS COVERING A CLAIM

Chicago and Great Northern Railroad Co.

Claim No. *419*
Amount *$230.00*

Commodity, *Green Fruit.* Claimant, *Fort Valley Commission Co.*
From *Winters, Cal.*, to *Oelwein, Iowa,* via *A. B. C. R. R.*
W/B *S. P. 65* Date *6/22/12* Car No. *X. Y. Z. 3031*

PERMIT INSPECTION PERISHABLE

B/L Instructions *Vents closed at Winters to Destination, car under ice from Winters, keep fully iced to destination.*
Cause and Basis of claim—*Fruit over-ripe, shows heavy shrinkage.*

Road	Station	Date	TIME In	Out	Ice	Temp.	VENTILATION W. Pipes	Plugs	Seals	Schedule Time Used	Delay
S. P.	*Winters*	*6/20*	*Car Ordered*								
		6/21	*Car Placed*								
		6/22	*Car Loaded*								
S. P.	*Winters*	*6/22*		*3:00 P. M.*	*11000*	*90* *88*					
	Roseville	*6/22*	*10:30 A. M.*	*11:00 A. M.*	*2000*	*79* *66*					
	Truckee	*6/24*	*11:30 P. M.*	*12:30 A. M.*	*1000*	*56* *32*					*6 hrs. 35 min.*
	Carlin	*6/24*	*8:25 A. M.*	*9:45 P. M.*		*72* *38*					
	Ogden	*6/25*	*11:15 A. M.*								
U. P.	*Ogden*	*6/25*		*1:05 P. M.*		*100* *60*	 *Open*	 *Closed*			
	Evanston	*6/25*	*8:15 P. M.*	*9:25 A. M.*	*2750*	*78* *43*	 *Open*	 *Closed*			
	N. Platte	*6/27*	*3:40 P. M.*	*4:45 P. M.*	*3440*		*Open*	*Closed*			
	Co. Bluffs	*6/28*	*5:50 A. M.*	*9:30 A. M.*		*100* *71*	 *Open*	 *Closed*			
C. & G. N.	*Co. Bluffs*	*6/29*	*9:30 P. M.*				*Open*	*Closed*			
	Oelwein	*6/29*	*11:35 A. M.*				*Open*	*One plug out in ice tank*			

20 boxes apricots and 80 boxes peaches over-ripe and mouldy.

Document 23

BRIEF

Claimant's bill attached calls for payment of $230.00 account alleged over-heated condition of the fruit at time consignment was delivered at Oelwein.

Outline shows movement of car from Winters, Calif., to Oelwein, Iowa, and statement of icing and temperature record. Car made very good time, being handled in seven days.

Car was iced by S. P. and U. P. at Winters, Roseville, Truckee, Evanston, and N. Platte. This company failed to ice while in its possession, although car was last iced at N. Platte about 10 P. M., June 27.

Agent of this company at Council Bluffs claims bunkers were 7/8 full at 9:30 A. M. the next morning.

Agent at Oelwein claims ice tanks were 1/2 full at time car arrived. It does seem that quantity of ice supplied while car was in transit ought to have maintained refrigeration throughout the journey.

The consignment checked out at Oelwein, 20 boxes apricots and 80 boxes peaches over-ripe and mouldy.

APPENDIX B

The primary object of this treatise has been to treat the subject of claims from the standpoint of the man who has already been damaged in some way in the handling of his freight, and who desires to know the proper method to be used in the collection of such damages from the carrier.

In the past, the energies of the carriers and the shippers have been very largely expended in the adjustment of claims after they have occurred. Within the last few years, however, there has been a very decided movement on the part of the carriers, the shippers, and the Interstate Commerce Commission to do what is possible to prevent claims. Some carriers now have special departments entirely devoted to the subject of investigating the causes of freight claims and suggesting measures by which the number and amount of claims may be materially reduced.

In making up Western Classification No. 51, the carriers had this point strongly in mind, and in many cases a change in rating was made so that it would be to the shipper's interest to take measures to ship his goods in such a way that the liability to claims would be materially reduced. The Interstate Commerce Commission strongly sanctions this action on the part of the carriers and, where it was shown that the difference in rating was based only on the desire of the carriers to reduce the amount of claims, the Commission allowed the higher rating on packages more liable to damage.

Much has been said and written on this subject and many valuable suggestions made. Space will not allow us to go into this subject in detail, but we give below some simple rules which if closely adhered to will materially assist in getting freight to destination without loss or damage. It should be borne in mind that, while carriers can be compelled to pay damage for which they are responsible, such payment will not reimburse the shipper for lost customers or other losses for which the carrier cannot be held. (See treatise on "Reducing Freight Charges to a Minimum.")

The suggestions given below are taken from the publication entitled, "Way to Ship," issued by the Chicago Association of Commerce.

Measures for Prevention of Claims

PACKING OF FREIGHT

(a) All package freight should be carefully and securely packed so as to be clearly able to withstand all ordinary risks of transportation. The use of flimsy packages and careless methods of packing should be avoided.

MARKING OF FREIGHT

(a) In the case of less carload shipments each package of freight should be legibly marked and so marked as not to be obliterated by ordinary risks of transportation. When necessary to use tags for marking, they should be strong and durable, made of rope, manila paper or linen and should be securely sewed to the package or tied to it by a wire tie.

(b) Name of consignee and destination in full. Where there are two points in a state of the same name, then the county should be designated.

(c) All old marks on packages should be removed or obliterated to avoid confusion as to which marks are correct.

(d) Wherever practicable shipper's name and location with the word "from" preceding them should be given.

If this is done, disposition of shipments which may go astray can be more readily accomplished.

BILLS OF LADING AND SHIPPING RECEIPTS

Bill of lading or shipping receipt should be made in a clear and legible manner, containing the following information in full:

(a) Name of shipping point and date of shipment.

(b) Name of consignor.

(c) Name of consignee and destination. Where there are two points in a state of the same name, then the county shall be designated.

(d) When the freight is consigned to a place not located on the line of a railroad, each package, bundle or piece shall be marked with the name of the station at which the consignee will accept delivery, and such other information given as required by the rules of the carriers.

(e) Number of packages and description of commodity.

(f) Less-than-carload freight shall be properly marked and special marks, if any, shown in shipping order or receipt.

NOTATION OF SHORTAGE AND DAMAGE ON FREIGHT BILLS

(a) Shortages discovered at time of delivery should be endorsed on the paid freight bill.

(b) Damages discovered at time of delivery should be endorsed upon the paid freight bill, such notation to state the exact extent and nature of damage.

APPENDIX C

CUMMINS AMENDMENT

Be it enacted by the Senate and House of Representatives of the United States of America in Congress assembled, That so much of section seven of an Act entitled "An Act to amend an Act entitled 'An Act to regulate commerce,' approved February fourth, eighteen hundred and eighty-seven, and all Acts amendatory thereof, and to enlarge the powers of the Interstate Commerce Commission," approved June twenty-ninth, nineteen hundred and six, as reads as follows, to wit:

"That any common carrier, railroad, or transportation company receiving property for transportation from a point in one State to a point in another State shall issue a receipt or a bill of lading therefor, and shall be liable to the lawful holder thereof for any loss, damage, or injury to such property caused by it or by any common carrier, railroad, or transportation company to which such property may be delivered, or over whose line or lines such property may pass, and no contract, receipt, rule, or regulation shall exempt such common carrier, railroad, or transportation company from the liability hereby imposed: *Provided,* That nothing in this section shall deprive any holder of such receipt or bill of lading of any remedy or right of action which he has under existing law," be, and the same is hereby, amended so as to read as follows, to wit:

"That any common carrier, railroad, or transportation company subject to the provisions of this Act receiving property for transportation from a point in one State or Territory or the District of Columbia to a point in another State, Territory, District of Columbia, or from any point in the United States to a point in an adjacent foreign country shall issue a receipt or bill of lading therefor, and shall be liable to the lawful holder thereof for any loss, damage, or injury to such property caused by it or by any common carrier, railroad, or transportation company to which such property may be delivered or over whose line or lines such property may pass within the United States or within an adjacent foreign country when transported on a through bill of lading, and no contract, receipt, rule, regulation, or other limitation of any character whatsoever, shall exempt such common carrier, railroad, or transportation company from the liability hereby imposed; and any such common carrier, railroad, or transportation company so receiving property for transportation from a point in one State, Territory, or the District of Columbia to a point in another State or Territory, or from a point in a State or Territory to a point in the District of Columbia, or from any point in the United States to a point in an adjacent foreign country, or for transportation wholly within a Territory shall be liable to the lawful holder of said receipt or bill of lading or to any party entitled to recover thereon, whether such receipt or bill of lading has been issued or not, for the full actual loss, damage, or injury to such property caused by it or by any such common carrier, railroad, or transportation company to which such property may be delivered or over whose line or lines such property may pass within the United States or within an adjacent foreign country when transported on a through bill of lading, notwithstanding any limitation of liability or limitation of the amount of recovery or representation or agreement as to value in any such receipt or bill of lading, or in any contract, rule, regulation, or in any tariff filed with the Interstate Commerce Commission; and any such limitation, without respect to the manner or form in which it is sought to be made is hereby declared to be unlawful and void. [1] "*Provided, however*, That the provisions hereof respecting liability for full actual loss, damage, or injury, notwithstanding any limitation of liability or recovery or representation or agreement or release as to value, and declaring any such limitation to be unlawful and void, shall not apply, first, to baggage carried on passenger trains or boats, or trains or boats carrying passengers; second, to property, except ordinary live stock, received for transportation concerning which the carrier shall have been or shall hereafter be expressly authorized or required by order of the Interstate Commerce Commission to establish and maintain rates dependent upon the value declared in writing by the shipper or agreed upon in writing as the released value of the property, in which case such declaration or agreement shall have no other effect than to limit liability and recovery to an amount not exceeding the value so declared or released, and shall not, so far as relates to values, be held to be a violation of section ten of this Act to regulate commerce, as amended; and any tariff schedule which may be filed with the commission pursuant to such order shall contain specific reference thereto and may establish rates varying with the value so declared or agreed upon; and the commission is hereby empowered to make such order in cases where rates dependent upon and varying with declared or agreed values would, in its opinion, be just and reasonable under the circumstances and conditions surrounding the transportation. The term 'ordinary live stock' shall include all cattle, swine, sheep, goats, horses, and mules, except such as are chiefly valuable for breeding, racing, show purposes, or other special uses." *Provided further*, That nothing in this section shall deprive any holder of such receipt or bill of lading of any remedy or right of action which he has under the existing law: *Provided further*, That it shall be unlawful for any such common carrier to provide by rule, contract, regulation, or otherwise a shorter period for giving notice of claims than ninety days and for the filing of claims for a shorter period than four months, and for the institution of suits than two years: *Provided, however*, That if the loss, damage, or injury complained of was due to delay or damage while being loaded or unloaded, or damaged in transit by carelessness or negligence, then no notice of claim nor filing of claim shall be required as a condition precedent to recovery."

[1]The following down to the words "Provided further, That nothing, etc.," is an amendment to Cummins' Amendment, which became effective August 9, 1916.

APPENDIX D

POMERENE BILL OF LADING LAW.

Be it enacted by the Senate and House of Rrepresentatives of the United States of America in Congress assembled, That bills of lading issued by any common carrier for the transportation of goods in any Territory of the United States, or the District of Columbia, or from a place in a State to a place in a foreign country, or from a place in one State to a place in another State, or from a place in one State to a place in the same State through another State or foreign country, shall be governed by this Act.

SEC. 2. That a bill in which it is stated that the goods are consigned or destined to a specified person is a straight bill.

SEC. 3. That a bill in which it is stated that the goods are consigned or destined to the order of any person named in such bill is an order bill. Any provision in such a bill or in any notice, contract, rule, regulation, or tariff that it is nonnegotiable shall be null and void and shall not affect its negotiability within the meaning of this Act unless upon its face and in writing agreed to by the shipper.

SEC. 4. That order bills issued in a State for the transportation of goods to any place in the United States on the Continent of North America, except Alaska and Panama, shall not be issued in parts or sets. If so issued, the carrier issuing them shall be liable for failure to deliver the goods described therein to anyone who purchases a part for value in good faith, even though the purchase be after the delivery of the goods by the carrier to a holder of one of the other parts: *Provided, however,* That nothing contained in this section shall be interpreted or construed to forbid the issuing of order bills in parts or sets for such transportation of goods to Alaska, Panama, Porto Rico, the Philippines, Hawaii, or foreign countries, or to impose the liabilities set forth in this section for so doing.

SEC. 5. That when more than one order bill is issued in a State for the same goods to be transported to any place in the United States on the Continent of North America, except Alaska and Panama, the word "duplicate," or some other word or words indicating that the document is not an original bill, shall be placed plainly upon the face of every such bill except the one first issued. A carrier shall be liable for the damage caused by his failure so to do to anyone who has purchased the bill for value in good faith as an original, even though the purchase be after the delivery of the goods by the carrier to the holder of the original bill: *Provided, however,* That nothing contained in this section shall in such case for such transportation of goods to Alaska, Panama, Porto Rico, the Philippines, Hawaii, or foreign countries be interpreted or construed so as to require the placing of the word "duplicate" thereon, or to impose the liabilities set forth in this section for failure so to do.

SEC. 6. That a straight bill shall have placed plainly upon its face by the carrier issuing it "nonnegotiable" or "not negotiable."

This section shall not apply, however, to memoranda or acknowledgments of an informal character.

SEC. 7. That the insertion in an order bill of the name of a person to be notified of the arrival of the goods shall not limit the negotiability of the bill or constitute notice to a purchaser thereof of any rights or equities of such person in the goods.

SEC. 8. That a carrier, in the absence of some lawful excuse, is bound to deliver goods upon a demand made either by the consignee named in the bill for the goods or, if the bill is an order bill, by the holder thereof, if such a demand is accompanied by—

(a) An offer in good faith to satisfy the carrier's lawful lien upon the goods;

(b) Possession of the bill of lading and an offer in good faith to surrender, properly indorsed, the bill which was issued for the goods, if the bill is an order bill; and

(c) A readiness and willingness to sign, when the goods are delivered, an acknowledgment that they have been delivered, if such signature is requested by the carrier.

In case the carrier refuses or fails to deliver the goods, in compliance with a demand by the consignee or holder so accompanied, the burden shall be upon the carrier to establish the existence of a lawful excuse for such refusal or failure.

SEC. 9. That a carrier is justified, subject to the provisions of the three following sections, in delivering goods to one who is—

(a) A person lawfully entitled to the possession of the goods, or

(b) The consignee named in a straight bill for the goods, or

(c) A person in possession of an order bill for the goods, by the terms of which the goods are deliverable to his order; or which has been indorsed to him, or in blank by the consignee, or by the mediate or immediate indorsee of the consignee.

SEC. 10. That where a carrier delivers goods to one who is not lawfully entitled to the possession of them, the carrier shall be liable to anyone having a right of property or possession in the goods if he delivered the goods otherwise than as authorized by subdivisions (b) and (c) of the preceding section; and, though he delivered the goods as authorized by either of said subdivisions, he shall be so liable if prior to such delivery he—

(a) Had been requested, by or on behalf of a person having a right of property or possession in the goods, not to make such delivery, or

(b) Had information at the time of the delivery that it was to a person not lawfully entitled to the possession of the goods.

Such request or information, to be effective within the meaning of this section, must be given to an officer or agent of the carrier, the actual or apparent scope of whose duties includes action upon such a request or information, and must be given in time to enable the officer or agent to whom it is given, acting with reasonable diligence, to stop delivery of the goods.

SEC. 11. That except as provided in section twenty-six, and except when compelled by legal process, if a carrier delivers goods for which an order bill had been issued, the negotiation of which would transfer the right to the possession of the goods, and fails to take up and cancel the bill, such carrier shall be liable for failure to deliver the goods to anyone who for value and in good faith purchases such bill, whether such purchaser acquired title to the bill before or after the delivery of the goods by the carrier and notwithstanding delivery was made to the person entitled thereto.

SEC. 12. That except as provided in section twenty-six, and except when compelled by legal process, if a carrier delivers part of the goods for which an order bill had been issued and fails either—

(a) To take up and cancel the bill, or

(b) To place plainly upon it a statement that a portion of the goods has been delivered with a description which may be in general terms either of the goods or packages that have been so delivered or of the goods or packages which still remain in the carrier's possession, he shall be liable for failure to deliver all the goods specified in the bill to anyone who for value and in good faith purchases it, whether such purchaser acquired title to it before or after the delivery of any portion of the goods by the carrier, and notwithstanding such delivery was made to the person entitled thereto.

SEC. 13. That any alteration, addition, or erasure in a bill after its issue without authority from the carrier issuing the same, either in writing or noted on the bill, shall be void, whatever be the nature and purpose of the change, and the bill shall be enforcible according to its original tenor.

SEC. 14. That where an order bill has been lost, stolen, or destroyed a court of competent jurisdiction may order the delivery of the goods upon satisfactory proof of such loss, theft, or destruction and upon the giving of a bond, with sufficient surety, to be approved by the court, to protect the carrier or any person injured by such delivery from any liability or loss incurred by reason of the original bill remaining outstanding. The court may also in its discretion order the payment of the carrier's reasonable costs and counsel fees: *Provided,* a voluntary indemnifying bond without order of court shall be binding on the parties thereto.

The delivery of the goods under an order of the court, as provided in this section, shall not relieve the carrier from liability to a person to whom the order bill has been or shall be negotiated for value without notice of the proceedings or of the delivery of the goods.

SEC. 15. That a bill, upon the face of which the word "duplicate" or some other word or words indicating that the document is not an original bill is placed, plainly shall impose upon the carrier issuing the same the liability of one who represents and warrants that such bill is an accurate copy of an original bill properly issued, but no other liability.

SEC. 16. That no title to goods or right to their possession asserted by a carrier for his own benefit shall excuse him from liability for refusing to deliver the goods according to the terms of a bill issued for them, unless such title or right is derived directly or indirectly from a transfer made by the consignor or consignee after the shipment, or from the carrier's lien.

SEC. 17. That if more than one person claim the title or possession of goods, the carrier may require all known claimants to interplead, either as a defense to an action brought against him for nondelivery of the goods or as an original suit, whichever is appropriate.

SEC. 18. That if some one other than the consignee or the person in possession of the bill has a claim to the title or possession of the goods, and the carrier has information of such claim, the carrier shall be excused from liability for refusing to deliver the goods, either to the consignee or person in possession of the bill or to the adverse claimant, until the carrier has had a reasonable time to ascertain the validity of the adverse claim or to bring legal proceedings to compel all claimants to interplead.

SEC. 19. That except as provided in the two preceding sections and in section nine, no right or title of a third person, unless enforced by legal process, shall be a defense to an action brought by the consignee of a straight bill or by the holder of an order bill against the carrier for failure to deliver the goods on demand.

SEC. 20. That when goods are loaded by a carrier such carrier shall count the packages of goods, if package freight, and ascertain the kind and quantity if bulk freight, and such carrier shall not, in such cases, insert in the bill of lading or in any notice, receipt, contract, rule, regulation, or tariff, "Shipper's weight, load, and count," or other words of like purport, indicating that the goods were loaded by the shipper and the description of them made by him or in case of bulk freight and freight not concealed by packages the description made by him. If so inserted, contrary to the provisions of this section, said words shall be treated as null and void and as if not inserted therein.

SEC. 21. That when package freight or bulk freight is loaded by a shipper and the goods are described in a bill of lading merely by a statement of marks or labels upon them or upon packages containing them, or by a statement that the goods are said to be goods of a certain kind or quantity, or in a certain condition, or it is stated in the bill of lading that packages are said to contain goods of a certain kind or quantity or in a certain condition, or that the contents or condition of the contents of packages are unknown, or words of like purport are contained in the bill of lading, such statements, if true, shall not make liable the carrier issuing the bill of lading, although the goods are not of the kind or quantity or in the condition which the marks or labels upon them indicate, or of the kind or quantity or in the condition they were said to be by the consignor. The carrier may also by inserting in the bill of lading the words "Shipper's weight, load, and count," or other words of like purport indicate that the goods were loaded by the shipper and the description of them made by him; and if such statement be true, the carrier shall not be liable for damages caused by the improper loading or by the non-receipt or by the misdescription of the goods described in the bill of lading: *Provided, however,* Where the shipper of bulk freight installs and maintains adequate facilities for weighing such freight, and the same are available to the carrier, then the carrier, upon written request of such shipper and when given a reasonable opportunity so to do, shall ascertain the kind and quantity of bulk freight within a reasonable time after such written request, and the carriers shall not in such cases insert in the bill of lading the words "Shipper's weight," or other words of like purport, and if so inserted contrary to the provisions of this section, said words shall be treated as null and void and as if not inserted therein.

SEC. 22. That if a bill of lading has been issued by a carrier or on his behalf by an agent or employee the scope of whose actual or apparent authority includes the receiving of goods and issuing bills of lading therefor for transportation in commerce among the several States and with foreign nations, the carrier shall be liable to (a) the owner of goods covered by a straight bill subject to existing right of stoppage in transit or (b) the holder of an order bill, who has given value in good faith, relying upon the description therein of the goods, for damages caused by the nonreceipt by the carrier of all or part of the goods or their failure to correspond with the description thereof in the bill at the time of its issue.

SEC. 23. That if goods are delivered to a carrier by the owner or by a person whose act in conveying the title to them to a purchaser for value in good faith would bind the owner, and an order bill is issued for them, they cannot thereafter, while in the possession of the carrier, be attached by garnishment or otherwise or be levied upon under an execution unless the bill be first surrendered to the carrier or its negotiation enjoined. The carrier shall in no such case be compelled to deliver the actual possession of the goods until the bill is surrendered to him or impounded by the court.

SEC. 24. That a creditor whose debtor is the owner of an order bill shall be entitled to such aid from courts of appropriate jurisdiction by injunction and otherwise in attaching such bill or in satisfying the claim by means thereof as is allowed at law or in equity in regard to property which can not readily be attached or levied upon by ordinary legal process.

SEC. 25. That if an order bill is issued the carrier shall have a lien on the goods therein mentioned for all charges on those goods for freight, storage, demurrage and terminal charges, and expenses necessary for the preservation of the goods or incident to their transportation subsequent to the date of the bill and all other charges incurred in transportation and delivery, unless the bill expressly enumerates other charges for which a lien is claimed. In such case there shall also be a lien for the charges enumerated so far as they are allowed by law and the contract between the consignor and the carrier.

SEC. 26. That after goods have been lawfully sold to satisfy a carrier's lien, or because they have not been claimed, or because they are perishable or hazardous, the carrier shall not thereafter be liable for failure to deliver the goods themselves to the consignee or owner of the goods, or to a holder of the bill given for the goods when they were shipped, even if such bill be an order bill.

SEC. 27. That an order bill may be negotiated by delivery where, by the terms of the bill, the carrier undertakes to deliver the goods to the order of a specified person, and such person or a subsequent indorsee of the bill has indorsed it in blank.

SEC. 28. That an order bill may be negotiated by the indorsement of the person to whose order the goods are deliverable by the tenor of the bill. Such indorsement may be in blank or to a specified person. If indorsed to a specified person, it may be negotiated again by the indorsement of such person in blank or to another specified person. Subsequent negotiation may be made in like manner.

SEC. 29. That a bill may be transferred by the holder by delivery, accompanied with an agreement, express or implied, to transfer the title to the bill or to the goods represented thereby. A straight bill cannot be negotiated free from existing equities, and the indorsement of such a bill gives the transferee no additional right.

SEC. 30. That an order bill may be negotiated by any person in possession of the same, however such possession may have been acquired, if by the terms of the bill the carrier undertakes to deliver the goods to the order of such person, or if at the time of negotiation the bill is in such form that it may be negotiated by delivery.

SEC. 31. That a person to whom an order bill has been duly negotiated acquires thereby—

(a) Such title to the goods as the person negotiating the bill to him had or had ability to convey to a purchaser in good faith for value, and also such title to the goods as the consignee and consignor had or had power to convey to a purchaser in good faith for value; and

(b) The direct obligation of the carrier to hold possession of the goods for him according to the terms of the bill as fully as if the carrier had contracted directly with him.

SEC. 32. That a person to whom a bill has been transferred, but not negotiated, acquires thereby as against the transferor the title to the goods, subject to the terms of any agreement with the transferor. If the bill is a straight bill such person also acquires the right to notify the carrier of the transfer to him of such bill and thereby to become the direct obligee of whatever obligations the carrier owed to the transferor of the bill immediately before the notification.

Prior to the notification of the carrier by the transferor or transferee of a straight bill the title of the transferee to the goods and the right to acquire the obligation of the carrier may be defeated by garnishment or by attachment or execution upon the goods by a creditor of the transferor, or by a notification to the carrier by the transferor or a subsequent purchaser from the transferor of a subsequent sale of the goods by the transferor.

A carrier has not received notification within the meaning of this section unless an officer or agent of the carrier, the actual or apparent scope of whose duties includes action upon such a notification, has been notified; and no notification shall be effective until the officer or agent to whom it is given has had time, with the exercise of reasonable diligence, to communicate with the agent or agents having actual possession or control of the goods.

SEC. 33. That where an order bill is transferred for value by delivery, and the indorsement of the transferor is essential for negotiation, the transferee acquires a right against the transferor to compel him to indorse the bill, unless a contrary intention appears. The negotiation shall take effect as of the time when the indorsement is actually made. This obligation may be specifically enforced.

SEC. 34. That a person who negotiates or transfers for value a bill by indorsement or delivery, unless a contrary intention appears, warrants—

(a) That the bill is genuine;

(b) That he has a legal right to transfer it.

(c) That he has knowledge of no fact which would impair the validity or worth of the bill;

(d) That he has a right to transfer the title to the goods, and that the goods are merchantable or fit for a particular purpose whenever such warranties would have been implied if the contract of the parties had been to transfer without a bill the goods represented thereby.

SEC. 35. That the indorsement of a bill shall not make the indorser liable for any failure on the part of the carrier or previous indorsers of the bill to fulfill their respective obligations.

SEC. 36. That a mortgagee or pledgee or other holder of a bill for security who in good faith demands or receives payment of the debt for which such bill is security, whether from a party to a draft drawn for such debt or from any other person, shall not be deemed by so doing to represent or warrant the genuineness of such bill or the quantity or quality of the goods therein described.

SEC. 37. That the validity of the negotiation of a bill is not impaired by the fact that such negotiation was a breach of duty on the part of the person making the negotiation, or by the fact that the owner of the bill was deprived of the possession of the same by fraud, accident, mistake, duress, loss, theft, or conversion, if the person to whom the bill was negotiated, or a person to whom the bill was subsequently negotiated, gave value therefor in good faith, without notice of the breach of duty, or fraud, accident, mistake, duress, loss, theft, or conversion.

SEC. 38. That where a person, having sold, mortgaged, or pledged goods which are in a carrier's possession and for which an order bill has been issued, or having sold, mortgaged, or pledged the order bill representing such goods, continues in possession of the order bill, the subsequent negotiation thereof by that person under any sale, pledge, or other disposition thereof to any person receiving the same in good faith, for value and without notice of the previous sale, shall have the same effect as if the first purchaser of the goods or bill had expressly authorized the subsequent negotiation.

SEC. 39. That where an order bill has been issued for goods no seller's lien or right of stoppage in transitu shall defeat the rights of any purchaser for value in good faith to whom such bill has been negotiated, whether such negotiation be prior or subsequent to the notification to the carrier who issued such bill of the seller's claim to a lien or right of stoppage in transitu. Nor shall the carrier be obliged to deliver or justified in delivering the goods to an unpaid seller unless such bill is first surrendered for cancellation.

SEC. 40. That, except as provided in section thirty-nine, nothing in this Act shall limit the rights and remedies of a mortgagee or lien holder whose mortgage or lien on goods would be valid, apart from this Act, as against one who for value and in good faith purchased from the owner, immediately prior to the time of their delivery to the carrier, the goods which are subject to the mortgage or lien and obtained possession of them.

SEC. 41. That any person who, knowingly or with intent to defraud, falsely makes, alters, forges, counterfeits, prints or photographs any bill of lading purporting to represent goods received for shipment among the several States or with foreign nations, or with like intent utters or publishes as true and genuine any such falsely altered, forged, counterfeited, falsely printed or photographed bill of lading, knowing it to be falsely altered, forged, counterfeited, falsely printed or photographed, or aids in making, altering, forging, counterfeiting, printing or photographing, or uttering or publishing the same, or issues or aids in issuing or procuring the issue of, or negotiates or transfers for value a bill which contains a false statement as to the receipt of the goods, or as to any other matter, or who, with intent to defraud, violates, or fails to comply with, or aids in any violation of, or failure to comply with any provision of this Act, shall be guilty of a misdemeanor, and, upon conviction, shall be punished for each offense by imprisonment not exceeding five years, or by a fine not exceeding $5,000, or both.

SEC. 42. First. That in this Act, unless the context of subject matter otherwise requires—

"Action" includes counterclaim, set-off, and suit in equity.

"Bill" means bill of lading governed by this Act.

"Consignee" means the person named in the bill as the person to whom delivery of the goods is to be made.

"Consignor" means the person named in the bill as the person from whom the goods have been received for shipment.

"Goods" means merchandise or chattels in course of transportation or which have been or are about to be transported.

"Holder" of a bill means a person who has both actual possession of such bill and a right of property therein.

"Order" means an order by indorsement on the bill.

"Person" includes a corporation or partnership, or two or more persons having a joint or common interest.

To "purchase" includes to take as mortgagee and to take as pledgee.

"State" includes any Territory, District, insular possession, or isthmian possession.

SEC. 43. That the provisions of this Act do not apply to bills made and delivered prior to the taking effect thereof.

SEC. 44. That the provisions and each part thereof and the sections and each part thereof of this Act are independent and severable, and the declaring of any provision or part thereof, or provisions or part thereof, or section or part thereof, or sections or part thereof, unconstitutional shall not impair or render unconstitutional any other provision or part thereof or section or part thereof.

SEC. 45. That this Act shall take effect and be in force on and after the first day of January next after its passage.

Approved, August 29, 1916.

Spotted something that isn't quite right?

Let us know and we'll fix it for future reprints.
And as a thank you for your diligence, we'll
send you a free Sothis book of your choice.

publisher@sothis.press

This page intentionally left blank

Except of course for that line above. And this one.
And whilst we have your attention, perhaps you'd
like to follow us on Instagram @sothis.press. Go on.

Made in United States
Cleveland, OH
09 November 2026

47955554R00049